D0906511

POCKET BOOK OF

RESILIENCE

First published in Great Britain 2019 by Trigger

Trigger is a trading style of Shaw Callaghan Ltd & Shaw Callaghan 23 USA, INC.

The Foundation Centre

Navigation House, 48 Millgate, Newark

Nottinghamshire NG24 4TS UK

www.triggerpublishing.com

British Library Cataloguing-in-Publication data

A CIP catalogue record for this book is available upon request
from the British Library

ISBN: 978-1-78956-138-8

Trigger Publishing has asserted their right under the Copyright,
Design and Patents Act 1988 to be identified as the author of this work

Cover design and typeset by Fusion Graphic Design Ltd.

Printed and bound in Dubai by Oriental Press

Paper from responsible sources

POCKET BOOK OF

RESILIENCE

www.triggerpublishing.com

the Shaw mind
FOUNDATION

Creating hope for children,
adults and families

INTRODUCTION

Modern life can be filled with so much: from the daily commute, a hectic schedule or cooking an evening meal; to those crucial turning points: quitting your job, moving house, finding love. Between the noise, it can be hard to find those all-important moments of quiet.

The Pocket Book of Resilience offers a little guidance for when the scales of life are tipped, times become turbulent and a moment of stillness is needed. From the minds of some of the world's most well-known figures, learn to find your footing, take a breath and stand on stable ground once more.

If you think you are too small
to make a difference, try sleeping
with a mosquito

Dalai Lama

I went through a long period where I
was afraid of doing things I wanted to do,
and you get your courage back,
which is what's important

George Michael

Resilience is not what happens to you.
It's how you react to, respond to, and recover
from what happens to you

Jeffrey Gitomer

The presence of evil was something to be first recognized, then dealt with, survived, outwitted, triumphed over

Toni Morrison

Only a man who knows what it
is like to be defeated can reach down to
the bottom of his soul and come ...

... up with the extra ounce of power
it takes to win when the match is even

Muhammad Ali

The greatest test of courage on Earth is to
bear defeat without losing heart

Robert Green Ingersoll

It's not the absence of fear.
It's overcoming it. Sometimes you've got
to blast through and have faith

Emma Watson

Part of being optimistic is keeping
one's head pointed toward the sun,
one's feet moving forward. ...

... There were many dark moments when my faith in humanity was sorely tested but I would not and could not give myself up to despair

Nelson Mandela

A hero is an ordinary individual who
finds the strength to persevere and endure in
spite of overwhelming obstacles

Christopher Reeve

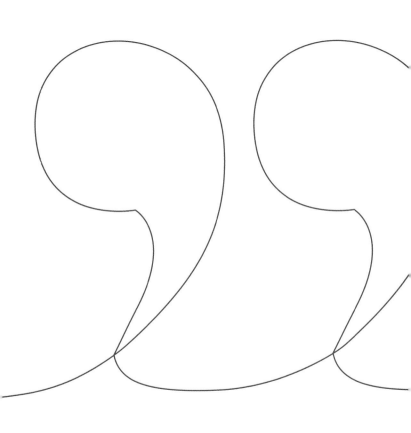

However difficult life may seem, there is always something you can do and succeed at

Stephen Hawking

Life is like riding a bicycle:
to keep your balance you
must keep moving

Albert Einstein

You can rise up from anything.
You can completely recreate yourself.
Nothing is permanent. You're not stuck.
You have choices. You can think new
thoughts. You can learn something new …

... You can create new habits.
All that matters is that you decide today
and never look back

Idil Ahmed

If the fire in your heart is strong enough,
it will burn away any obstacles that
come your way

Suzy Kassem

If you're walking down the right path
and you're willing to keep walking,
eventually you'll make progress

Barack Obama

You have to stop crying, and you
have to go kick some ass

Lady Gaga

I am the underdog, and I want to prove that one can follow one's dreams despite all the flaws and setbacks

Winnie Harlow

Be thankful for the hard times,
for they have made you

Leonardo DiCaprio

Be true to your heart ... put your whole heart and soul into it, and then whatever you do, it will shine through

Jamie Brewer

People who wonder whether the
glass is half empty or half full miss the point.
The glass is refillable

Anonymous

It's a journey, and the sad thing
is you only learn from experience:
so as much as someone
can tell you things ...

... you have to go out there
and make your own mistakes
in order to learn

Emma Watson

You can go a month without food,
you can live three days without water,
but you can't go more than sixty
seconds without hope

Sean Swarner

Do not pray for an easy life, pray for the strength to endure a difficult one

Bruce Lee

Sometimes, things may not
go your way, but the effort should be
there every single night

Michael Jordan

I've never walked away from anything
– and I'm not going to start now

Karren Brady

We fall. We break. We fail.
But then, we rise. We heal.
We overcome

Kiana Azizian

Tragedy should be utilized
as a source of strength. No matter
what sort of difficulties, how painful
experience is, if we lose our hope,
that's our real disaster

Dalai Lama

Whether you come from
a council estate or a country estate,
your success will be determined by your
own confidence and fortitude

Michelle Obama

If you can't fly then run, if you can't run then walk, if you can't walk then crawl, but whatever you do you have to keep moving forward

Martin Luther King Jr.

Everyone can rise above their
circumstances and achieve success
if they are dedicated to and passionate
about what they do

Nelson Mandela

Only you and you alone can
change your situation. Don't blame
it on anything or anyone

Leonardo DiCaprio

I've missed more than 9000 shots
in my career. I've lost almost 300 games.
26 times, I've been trusted to take the
game-winning shot and missed ...

... I've failed over and over and over again in my life. And that's why I succeed

Michael Jordan

Remember that sometimes,
not getting what you want is a
wonderful stroke of luck

Dalai Lama

I know what I can do so
it doesn't bother me what
other people think or their
opinion on the situation

Usain Bolt

Whenever you have a goal,
whether you want to be a doctor
or a singer, people will find a way
to bring you down ...

... I always tell people that if you have something you're really passionate about, don't let anyone tell you that you can't do it

Selena Gomez

Different is good.
When someone tells you that
you are different, smile and hold
your head up and be proud

Angelina Jolie

Hate no one, no matter how much they've wronged you. Live humbly, no matter how wealthy you become. Think positively, no matter how hard life is. Give much, even if you've been given little ...

... Forgive all, especially yourself. And never stop praying for the best for everyone

Imam

If I cannot do great things,
I can do small things in a great way

Martin Luther King Jr.

All the people who knock me down,
only inspire me to do better

Selena Gomez

It's only a bad day, not a bad life

Anonymous

There are two ways to go when you
hit a crossroads in your life:
There is the bad way, when you sort of
give up, and then there is the really
hard way, when you fight back ...

... I went the hard way and came out of it ok. Now I'm sitting here and doing great

Matthew Perry

You'll never do a whole lot unless
you're brave enough to try

Dolly Parton

Who cares what people think? Just believe
in yourself. That's all that matters

Britney Spears

Falling down is an accident.
Staying down is a choice.

Rosemary Nonny Knight

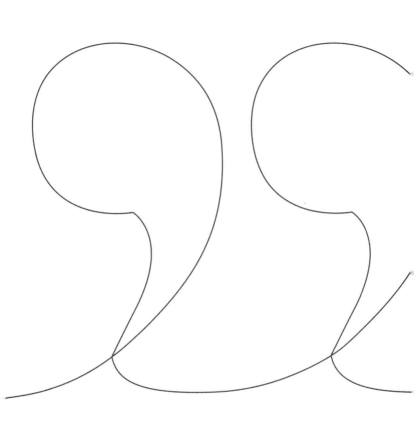

Someone was hurt before you,
wronged before you, hungry before you,
frightened before you, beaten before you,
humiliated before you, raped before you ...

... yet, someone survived.
You can do anything you choose to do

Maya Angelou

Whatever words we utter should
be chosen with care, for people will hear
them and be influenced by them ...

... for good or ill

Buddha

First principle: never to let one's self be beaten down by persons or by events

Marie Curie

The thing you fear most has no power.
Your fear of it is what has the power.
Facing the truth really will set you free

Oprah Winfrey

All those things that you're worried about
are not important. You're going to be OK.
Better than OK. You're going to be great.
Spend less time tearing yourself apart,
worrying if you're good enough ...

... You are good enough. And you're going to meet amazing people in your life who will help you and love you

Reese Witherspoon

I allow myself to fail.
I allow myself to break.
I'm not afraid of my flaws

Lady Gaga

Resilience is accepting your new reality, even if it's less good than the one you had before. You can fight it, you can do nothing but scream about what you've lost ...

... or you can accept that and try to put together something that's good

Elizabeth Edwards

I count him braver who
overcomes his desires than him
who conquers his enemies ...

... for the hardest victory is over the self

Aristotle

My barn having burned down,
I can now see the moon

Mizuta Masahide

If your heart is broken,
make art with the pieces

Shane Koyczan

Resilience is very different than being numb.
Resilience means you experience, you feel,
you fail, you hurt. You fall. But, you keep going

Yasmin Mogahed

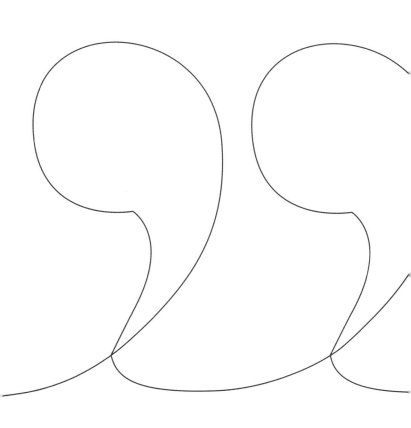

To be rendered powerless does not destroy
your humanity. Your resilience is your
humanity. The only people who lose their
humanity are those who believe they
have the right to render another human
being powerless ...

... They are the weak.
To yield and not break,
that is incredible strength

Hannah Gadsby

Only those who dare to fail greatly,
can ever achieve greatly

Robert F. Kennedy

Out of suffering have emerged the strongest souls; the most massive characters are seared with scars

Kahlil Gibran

The best people possess a feeling
for beauty, the courage to take risks,
the discipline to tell the truth,
the capacity for sacrifice ...

... Ironically, their virtues make them vulnerable; they are often wounded, sometimes destroyed

Ernest Hemingway

Rock bottom became the solid
foundation on which I rebuilt my life

J.K. Rowling

It's during our very worst fall that we
can either die or learn to fly

Sira Masetti

What would life be if we had
no courage to attempt anything?

Vincent Van Gogh

You will have bad times, but they
will always wake you up to the
stuff you weren't paying attention to

Robin Williams

Success isn't always about
'greatness', it's about consistency.
Consistent, hard work gains success.
Greatness will come

Dwayne "The Rock" Johnson

The strongest oak of the forest
is not the one that is protected from the
storm and hidden from the sun.
It's the one that stands in the open ...

... where it is compelled to struggle for its existence against the winds and rains and the scorching sun

Napoleon Hill

To be nobody but yourself in a world
that's doing its best to make you somebody
else is to fight the hardest battle you are ever
going to fight. Never stop fighting

E.E. Cummings

Life opens up opportunities to you,
and you either take them or you
stay afraid of taking them

Jim Carrey

It's a slow process,
but quitting won't speed it up

Anonymous

I just feel like there is nothing I cannot do

Stormzy

You've got enemies?
Good; that means you actually
stood up for something

Winston Churchill

There's no shame in failing.
The only shame is not giving
things your best shot

Robin Williams

We ourselves feel that we
are a drop in the ocean. But the
ocean would be less because
of that missing drop

Mother Teresa

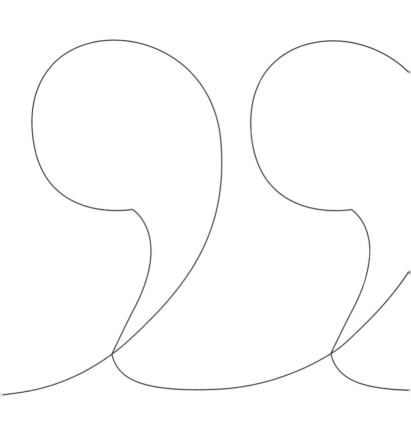

Life can be much broader once
you discover one simple fact:
Everything around you that you call life
was made up by people that were no
smarter than you. And you can change it,
you can influence it ...

... Once you learn that,
you'll never be the same again

Steve Jobs

There's no such thing as ruining your life.
Life's a pretty resilient thing, it turns out

Sophie Kinsella

Life may try to knock you down
but be persistent with your passions
and cultivate grit, resilience, tenacity and
endurance, success will come

Amit Ray

Every single thing that I was told that I couldn't do without a label – get in the charts, get on to the Radio 1 playlist – I've done

Stormzy

Resiliency is something you do,
more than something you have ...

... You become highly resilient by continuously learning your best way of being yourself in your circumstance

Al Siebert

Never be ashamed of a scar;
it simply means you were stronger than
whatever tried to hurt you

Demi Lovato

It is better to risk starving to death
than surrender. If you give up on your
dreams, what's left?

Jim Carrey

I realised that I don't
have to be perfect.
All I have to do is show up
and enjoy the messy ...

... imperfect and beautiful
journey of my life

Kerry Washington

It's not stress that kills us;
it is our reaction to it.
Adopting the right attitude ...

... can convert a negative stress
into a positive one

Hans Selye

My focus is to forget the pain of life.
Forget the pain, mock the pain, reduce it.
And laugh

Jim Carrey

Life is not a matter of holding good cards,
but of playing a poor hand well

Robert Louis Stevenson

The only way to make sense
out of change is to plunge into it,
move with it, and join the dance

Alan Watts

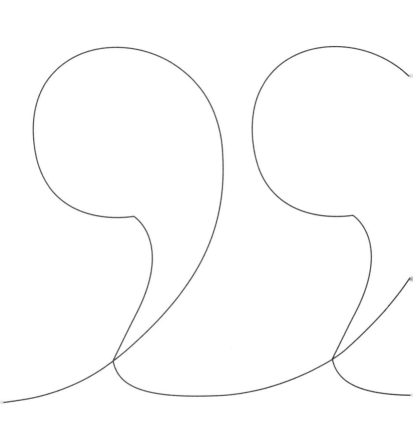

Our greatest glory is not
in never falling, but in rising
every time we fall

Confucius

Sometimes you just gotta
let shit go and say 'To hell with it'
and move on

Eminem

123

Change what you can,
manage what you can't

Raymond McCauley

Resilience is knowing that you are the
only one that has the power ...

... and the responsibility to pick yourself up

Mary Holloway

Things always get better
with time, just wait and see

Clavel Nelson

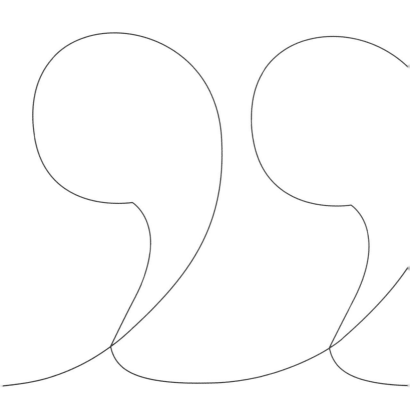

My scars remind me that I did indeed
survive my deepest wounds.
That in itself is an accomplishment.
And they bring to mind something else, too.
They remind me that the damage life has
inflicted on me has, in many places ...

... left me stronger and more resilient. What hurt me in the past has actually made me better equipped to face the present

Steve Goodier

I like to use the hard times in
the past to motivate me today

Dwayne "The Rock" Johnson

Although the world is full of suffering,
it is also full of the overcoming of it

Helen Keller

One's dignity may be assaulted,
vandalized and cruelly mocked,
but it can never be taken away
unless it is surrendered.

Michael J. Fox

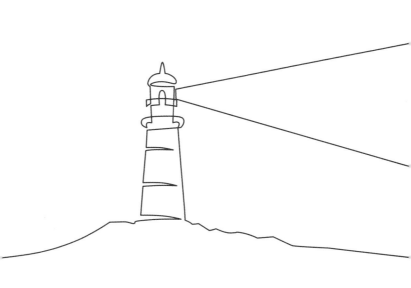

Sadness gives depth.
Happiness gives height. Sadness gives roots.
Happiness gives branches.
Happiness is like a tree going into the sky,
and sadness is like the roots going down
into the womb of the earth. Both are needed,
and the higher a tree goes ...

... the deeper it goes, simultaneously. The bigger the tree, the bigger will be its roots. In fact, it is always in proportion. That's its balance.

Osho

Learn what is to be taken
seriously and laugh at the rest

Herman Hesse

We will either find a way, or make one

Hannibal Barca

No matter how much falls on us,
we keep ploughing ahead. That's the only
way to keep the roads clear

Greg Kincaid

Every morning we are born again.
What we do today is what matters most

Buddha

The moment we believe that success is determined by an ingrained level of ability as opposed to resilience and hard work, we will be brittle in the face of adversity

Joshua Waitzkin

There comes a time in your life when you walk away from all the drama and people who create it. You surround yourself with people who make you laugh. Forget the bad and focus on the good. Love the people who treat you right ...

... pray for the ones who do not. Life is too short to be anything but happy. Falling down is a part of life, getting back up is living

José N. Harris

For a little guidance elsewhere ...

POCKET BOOK OF

COMPASSION

For when life gets a little tough

POCKET BOOK OF
WISDOM

For when life gets a little tough

POCKET BOOK OF

BALANCE

For when life gets a little tough

www.triggerpublishing.com

Trigger is a publishing house devoted to opening conversations about mental health. We tell the stories of people who have suffered from mental illnesses and recovered, so that others may learn from them.

www.shawmindfoundation.org

We aim to end the suffering and despair caused by mental health issues. Our goal is to make help and support available for every single person in society, from all walks of life. We will never stop offering hope. These are our promises.